Gradual Rea

Kali Ri

Published by Nine Pens

2021

www.ninepens.co.uk

ISBN: 978-1-8384321-3-3

004

Contents

After the Eruption

there was beauty of a kind that could not be easily
perceived from the ground. Those fissures of terror
were the craquelure glaze on the ancient vase
forged from earth, finished with fire. This land too is fire
kissed. Only nature remains. Not the bucolic green
of over-worked fields, nor their sensible grids
corralled by barbed wire. But the reaching of fault
lines, spider fingers of Mother, the flute of rising
song, the falsetto of combustion, the release of drawing
unconscious, unleashing convulsions. Nature
as in ochre, as in umber, as in charcoal, as in iron,
as in mushroom, as in ossein, as in bark, as in leaf
mulch. Ruination so rich it gifts mouth-
to-mouth nourishment. In the stolid blink of her eye
the embers teem with life, life as even we know it.

There are crows in the river

— They're swimming, love. Having such fun.
(rigor mortis backstroke in rusty water)

A sprightly current has them wheeling, but the depths
hunch archaic, observe with vast grievous eye.

We're safe on the bridge: bastion of civilisation.
So sturdy it's hard to believe it evanescent.

How sweet to be four, if we plunge into the abyss
he says we'll regenerate at level one.

I lift him, hold him tight – this moment eternal,
like the trinkets of dog shit hanging from low branches.

Swimming crows mean witches live here.

And we trail them, those herbal hags,
bearing mark of the beast, damning clitoral teat;

atop medieval stone path, splintering planks,
beneath finger locked branches, through haze of nettles.

We hurl spearheads into the gorge from the iron age fort;
only ten thousand years old, mere babe of stone.

All the while the corvids are gathering, cackling.
All the while they lament their lost.

Singing crows mean witches ceased here.

We eschew dubious woodpeckers, instead dash
histrionic, devour imagination, drain mine dry.

This walk eternal, will it never end –
lure him back with promise of plastic-wrapped crap.

Race you to the car; who's going to win?
(*not I*, hiss the naiads, ossified into silt)

Perspective

Giant among the newly planted
saplings, I do not think of their inherent
potential, but of Perpendicular Gothic
masters, men whom I insult
by imagining them heretical wizards
summoning Titans
to hold up domed ceilings,
commanding armies of ants
to chisel through Gaia's intestines,
haul gleaming kidneys and golden glands
and ribbons of veins to capitulate
before robe kissed feet, consuming
lifetimes to create vaulted portals
between clay fatality and celestial possibility;
Helios, at their say so, igniting stained faith,
bolstering bipedal entitlement, for O it is ours
for the taking, conducts this epoch
of impact, sings the Anthropocene chorus,
and while my ears ring and my lips
trill, the root of the ancient chestnut
convulses, cheese wire through soil,
lands clean under my jaw,
neck snaps back, and hell,
it just keeps going up, all rattlesnake
screaming leaves, all sinew
of the Gods, spine twisting
as this Behemoth circles in slow, slow
horror.

Betterment

The deer are startled, bolt-holes
clagged up with newspaper; periphery
patrolled by swinging axes hosting
Disney sing-alongs.
Their home harvested – birch
boiled soft then topped with red
brick duplications.

The animal charity isn't interested.
Vermin, they say, shoot them,
they suggest. Bring back wolves
and lynx, the rewilding enthusiasts
counter. Next morning,
three flattened hedgehogs mar
the road. Fledglings play with cats.

Revert

it is not as you remember
but some essence remains that evokes
single digits   the wealth in the walls
loom with authority
shrinking you into jelly sandals
that blue jumper with the horse
and its lack of city
noises   vehicles electric burr
obnoxious voices   opens space
for necromancy and play
you can transform
into a fox   silken streak
of hunted creature
slip through the 16th century
village   autumnal leaf wind-hauled
past the graveyard where dad
is buried   buried but not listening
until the lung-aching intake
of sewn miles   until the glutted knoll
of pine   where scent marks spell
welcome   and roots grasp limbs
like cousins at a funeral
and the air is thick with malaise   rank
with the mad barking
of approaching hounds   snapping
you back   into that vertical frame

Vulpes vulpes

It is ironic, I suppose, that here, so much closer
to the countryside, the end of this road flanked
by fields, grain stretching monotonous,
overlooked by kestrels, I have yet to see a single fox.

Though I have compiled enough evidence, mostly strewn
rubbish, to believe my daily steps overlap their subtle
tread, and as field effluvium seeps into the house,
I note your thick musk among the sour manure.

My road is named after them, and after their dwelling,
in that strange affliction we have of bestowing
upon settlements the title of that which we have destroyed.
Fifty years ago this was a tenebrous forest of oak and beech.

I miss urban foxes as I miss you.
Nocturnal dart of red leaving eyes hungering for the maw
of nature, the soothing of myth. Aristotle placed us
closest to divinity, believing humans imbued with light

and air, while foxes were earth and bone.
But you and me both are earth types, and you are now clean
bones. How I long to dig beneath those final damning months.
To nose the soil and speak gentle to your skeleton.

Leviathan

Her press of fluid flesh, boundless fingers probing
febrile against a chokehold of grey mortar—boiling,

she nuzzles with the affection of a cat in a nest.
Her vast breath drapes the fens, exhales from churned

peat bogs, cascades down scorched moors. Singular
entity devoured by arrogance of vampyre, contaminated

by agriculture, by stagnant filmy apathy, pissed
and shat out, and now, it is her time to feast;

to pop slick bones into tectonic joints,
reabsorb/reconnect into multifaceted beast.

You know her as pervasive miasma of creeping unease,
worming the wood soft and disintegrating crops;

as sluggish propulsion, opaque with corruption;
snow globe of microplastics infusing the sediment.

Just wait until she crests.

All vagaries of seascapes, all troposphere mercurial,
all purple surge horizon, all steaming tempest maelstrom.

Behold the phantasmal renegade
swallowing cities into sand.

Feather

Glint of blue plumage trills; luminous shaft
conjoined to the grey of coming storms.
Don't touch it, I warned the kids

when they were relentless, guidance
replacing conversation, leaving me
struggling to converse with adults,

to not raise my voice in a soaring lilt.
But now I walk alone; my own hand less
precious. *Parasites, bacteria, viruses*

do not quell me. I pick it up, admire
the oil slick surface; cool amethyst
drifting into voltaic sapphire. Countless

others protrude from the litter-strewn
verge, blanketing earth in vulnerable
down. Has a massacre occurred; an urban

shooting; a training for dog fights;
an augur reading doom? Or am I simply
mouthing dandelion for the very first time –

See how it looks like a lion? Concealed
in plain sight, veiled behind glut, overlooked by a single, dispassionate gull.

Toil

wake to dust motes in sunbeams
convincing surge in dopamine

O radiance
O hope

stand here bathed in honied light
regarding the stones

pebbles rubble boulders
igneous sedimentary meta–
morphic

pick them up one by one
pile them into a trembling tower

a dry stone wall
a ring of fortitude

a cairn of memorial
slate bone stack

precarious anatomy skeletal remains
of the *lovely* then the defiled then the punished
Medusa

no head
(press your forehead to the dirt in sororal deference)

pause

when her dust rises in cylindrical whirls
spitting grit into your eyes

O beautiful day

rebuild rearrange reassemble
think yourself sculptor modernist abstractor

see here
these rocks germinating smallest to largest
– manifestation of ennui

and here
does this cascade not sing impermanence

there is romance in this labour
not object but shape

termite mounds mammalian dens
sleeping forms ensconced by time

reminiscent of waking each morning
to liver grown anew

Ebb and Flow

A pike – so large it's difficult to fathom
such a brute patrolling this meagre brown slip –
lurks in a dank corner of concrete drainage,
trapped when the floodwater receded.

A mink, descended from escapees who slipped
unctuous from fur farms in the 70s, can't believe
her luck on finding the seething fish, three times
her size but helpless against tooth and claw.

The last of this region's water voles ticks
in his burrow, not soothed by the stink of scales
turning, nor realising the hum intoning brief
respite, but winding down both grass and time.

Wasting

sacral

       central sinking   musty rise

creaking   lumpen   past it   time

for a new one

       what of this one

with its rips   stains   horror   beneath

the topper   admission of animal

       instinctual lusts   supine ooze

fever   sweats

lunar   propulsion of plasma   post-

partum bleeding   leaking breasts souring

      rejection of watery   foremilk

expulsion of nutritious   hindmilk

base   claw torn   yellowed

      did you ever truly gleam

      did you sit in a showroom   a gallery

among detritus   dividing passing eyes

         nothing   lasts

you and I both   destined

     to fester   at the tip

burn   at the   incinerator

why   hold on   clutching

    familiarity   comfort

our visceral family   history

     longing to meld

flesh to fabric   in the mire

Dethroned

There are no seals here.
The blogs promised doleful faces
washed up on the shore, beached
and benevolent water puppies. I think
I want to see them for me. I worry
I only want to vaunt
that I've seen them.

Retreat and the coast shifts
into a deathscape,
all the soft whimsy flattened
by the fast-approaching iron tide.
A choice: walk slowly through the swarms
of flies, so thick my legs carve
the fetor of rotting blubber;
or give into instinct, run
so the flies balloon into thunderous clouds,
run and risk falling, risk splitting open
knees and palms on ridged ammonite curls, blood
infusing with the phantom, stinking past.

In the distance we play, all vulnerable
and godly, in plastic clothes with plastic
toys, in the tranquil idyll of the victor.

This used to be their kingdom.

Vicissitude

Streaks of green have me commenting with graceless
awe. Yes, I'm unsettled by the sheen of emerald birds

against this leaden backdrop, the fug now visible, though
growing up I could not see it. Thirty years in this city

and everything about its rapid psyche whirring was normal.
Three years gone and I'm wading through miasma

of spectres, all those gin-soaked mothers, the debtors'
prison runners. You've yet to join the current familial

exodus so betray no surprise. They're everywhere,
you don't say, because didn't we track their haunting

in shared emergence, our feathers salient in brilliant pink.
Under the silence of mourning we watch them cluster

in a plane, the tree clever enough to shed pollution with
its bark, and I think, I used to be able to do that, but now

look at me, wheezing, waxen, aiming my camera like a
tourist. Listen, you say, and they shriek in messianic tones,

reminiscent of parents soaked and running/reminiscent
of bygone twilight walks wedged between canal and zoo.

Heirlooms

Presently, the fish will again
flop terra firma, a coordinated
mass, spinning murmurations.

This island, a landing strip with an x
at its heart, surrounded by undulating
sea monsters, flattened by gales.

The saplings have long ceased trying.
x marks an epoch's mass grave.
x is a femur crossed with a humerus.

And still there are sharks, playing
with our remains: darting shoals
of synthesis—who will outlast who.

Next Summer

And we were warned by ghoulish algorithms, by friends
who used to be radical, and though we laughed as we

teetered across this airbed land, we knew them to be
right when our pegs were consumed by soil accustomed

to the taste of rogue metal, yet still we remarked that
the lopsided tent would do, and still we breathed in rot

and claimed it ambrosia, and once dark – kindling
moist and extinguishing – crawled into the plastic mouth

and lay on the ripe floor, waking throughout the night,
each time a little deeper, a little closer to her heart, eyes

taking in more oblivion than we could stand, yet we kept
terror internal, allowed fungus to spread between fingers

and toes, did not roll away from the nudging of curious
worms. Did we think our stoicism would be rewarded?

That she would call back the rabid waves, the straining
clouds, the porcine rivers, the relentless winds?

First light, gasping rebirth, we pushed out of the sucker
punch mud – ephemeral animals of clay, so easily dissolved.

Your heavy body bears down,
though too much earth rots flesh, so I sit you on a plinth
of carpet, and disconnected, your vines reach out, spread
into a web of smaller tendrils, gripping grass like a baby
holding a finger. You were planted by me, began life
on a windowsill in a plastic propagator
in a house heated by the burning of fossil fuels,
and when big enough were transported here via rickety pram,
its last journey before the tip, its last cradling
of new and hopeful life. You were replanted by bare hands,
fingernails encrusted with soil and much needed microbes;
and now you grow obscure/obscene.
I daily catch sight of your pregnant stretch, belly of seeds,
but where does your brain reside – do I admire an egg,
a glimpse of midriff? I know that your mouth gaping with thirst
hides under the invasive couch grass, weeds
that I cannot pull up without snapping your spiral fingers,
without thinking of babies left crying until they learn
that no one will come. Each day I tuck you in, gentle but firm.
For what? A single evening of decoration, an anthropogenic
celebration, scooping out your innards, carving your skin.
And for weeks to follow collapsed carcasses line forests, blight
beauty spots, stink the parks with sweet rot – left
by people absolving their guilt by feeding the squirrels,
until they read that you're harmful to hedgehogs
whose numbers are in decline, and are momentarily shamed,
momentarily regretful.

Reap

The eight-year-old is learning about rainforests.
We bring up page after page of luscious green –
it's all red-eyed tree frogs and fantastical toucans
and plants sped up seeking amber pools of light.

There are no bulldozers.

No jaguar's paw
sat lonely, dismembered
in a field recently cleared by chains
to plant soya beans.

Terra Incognita

Daughter of decompose. They laugh at you,
with your handfuls of loam, spreading leaf rot
beneath withered trees. See how your cheeks erupt red.
You belong north of here. You have a climb looming
and a body ill-suited to it. The stallions
are run through with metal, circled by iron.
What is a witch except a woman
who knows her plants. What is a witch except a girl
who courts the devil. You're halfway there.
That leaves fall with purpose is obvious,
not learned. Dig enough holes and you'll find the bones
of wolves, of lynx, even of bears. Gravel is agony
for unclad feet. The devil can innovate
to these climes, the witch cannot. The devil remains
necessary, his door open to those who rap out the correct
sequence. See how his followers pray, chins tucked into necks,
eyes rolling back in heads, smelling of sharp decline.
Curl your toes, seek the welcome of soil. The white mares
have yellowed, bloated with fug. Foliage from towering
planes fills the lightwell, climbs the windows like damp.
From this basement bedroom you track their slow deterioration.
You pretend to be a fox, mouth wetting at the writhe of worms
against glass. Watch the leaves yield splayed fingers
to the mastication of terrestrial invertebrates.
Press your hand to the pane and feel heat—
it is a misconception that death must be cold.

Annex

I thought I would make friends at the pottery class.

Her career, exemplifying Modernism, spanned five decades.
leading / avant-garde / direct carving

Will the clay run out? I worried as the binbag filled up.

I took you to the Hepworth gallery in Wakefield, and
you said you could imagine leaving London.

Where does it come from? Earth, yes, but the exact details
remain mystery; my usual curiosity dampened by fear..

– relationship between the human figure and the landscape –

..of facing mass waste. The frivolity of *hobbies*.

Key works: Mother and Child 1934 –

At this narrow point of modernity the Calder evokes
Regent's Canal. How we walked Camden to Angel, week..

– '..the vacant space in the centre of the mother's body'

..after week, pushing prams, cradling our precious babes.

Why St. Ives? Do the Pennines not thrash in wild beauty?

Each Wednesday evening, two hours of reticence
among noise; my hands shaping headless women.

– Pierced Hemisphere II 1937-8.

How scenic, our drive – Area of Outstanding Natural
Beauty. Brimham Rocks: formed 325 million years ago.

"When they are in special accord.. ..a child in the womb..
..one senses the architecture of bones in the human..."

Does the idol stone not look crafted by hands?
Formed for druidic worship? It inspired her, surely?

Calder: *hard or violent water* in early Common Brittonic.

My thumbs pressing wide hips, pinching forth breasts.

Sandstone quarried at Coldstones: unfathomably old –
peer down at the vacant space pertaining to our loss.

Unearthed

Here lies the sylvan cave coiled by exposed roots,
where time is resurrected – you cannot but think of this opening
as sealed, firmed by carapace of two meter fertility,
wadding of moss, the downward thrust of tree. And deeper
the firm clink of stone, excavated by footfall,
skaithed by hail. Here the hyena bones rest undisturbed.
Remember, she says, and speaks again of the algae
you mistook for grass which was in fact glass,
the viscous kind that drags you right down.
Such terror to fall through what you believe
to be solid. She steps into the cave,
demonstrates that she too knows of the sheath
between worlds. Here lingers a vestige of primalwoman
tonguing the perplexity of plants. She grinds up the lotus
which coughs chemical spores, and you see a shadow
of resemblance, familial linking between her face and —

Barren

Sharp contraction
as earth breathes in then holds that breath;
the diver submerged for so long
we presume her dead.
Shark food,
scattershot of matter sinking deeper than cameras.
The ring in the ice abandoned;
we let it close over like a gummy scab.

Fill our homes with tallow flicker –
atrophic wardens of inertia.
Oh these hardened days of pervasive gloom;
lungs filled with mortar.
None will see her emerge,
eyes sealed shut,
skin terribly puckered,
green shoots thrusting from bone.

Visitors from Scandinavia

High-pitched calls peal through the darkness.
The redwings are arriving,
cresting easterly winds
on the misted breath of rain.

The first of the winter thrushes,
UK conservation status: red;
highest threat, requiring urgent action.
I press my hand to the glass all night

and watch. Does this help? I ask aloud—
it's all I can do when my children
ride their bikes on the road
and wade into rivers, clamber up trees.

I watched as my firstborn fell
from the bough of Highgate's oldest oak;
watched a friend carry her and flag down a taxi,
my eyes straining in quiet horror,

thinking, it's too late, the damage
is already done. But it was only a broken elbow,
only five weeks in a cast, no code red,
no depleting undertaking surging towards defeat.

Night Soaked

Soft touch   astride a bridge and on a cheek
   not from he who begrudges your ripening
but hesitant reaching   but love

You have the hands of a primordial woman
perpetual motion   working working into fists

Does a fable exist more poignant
than hunger   swimming back through rivulets
of blood   to soak in the bog of *need*

Human skin   naturally water resistant
you should not fear the deluge
   unless longing to feel   nothing

Hot tongue on your eye encouraging *sight*
   for atheists it pains us to believe in Paradise Lost

Beneath this bridge lurk trolls   wearing parental
masks   their approval not required
your genesis meaningless   a fuck

Cold hands on your chest refuse the flush to rise
no shame in being animal   being hormones
   throbbing urges

The weight of embrace betrays fear
betrays stones in your pockets

the fallen woman   a Victorian ideal
neoteric expressions glut the zeitgeist

The flesh is weak   the mind weaker
you scorn o' th' milk of human kindness

Scream the river stinks   the air stinks   sewage
and shit and industry and cancer
   constant anxiety of peripheral strobes
undulating drone of parasitic wasps

Press my breast to your breast
   mammary mamma
                    milc supping mammal
literal elixir   derided   sexualised

The weight of embrace   heavier when engorged
the bridge isn't swaying
   I'm here   I'm here

Mother

found soil of sand
meshed in landscape of boreal tones
unmistakably the northern wild

demise coating the bleached grass
in humps of scorched gorse
in skeletal failed trees

to see for unhindered miles
and know disease utterly
imbedded   oh child

she said to the withered moss
to the gasping dust whorls
before leaning into ancient stone

of blackened slate
whose exposed spine
mirrored the coils

of fist clench rain clouds
anguish prowling the sky
fall here she soothed

and opened her mouth
let us swell   churn up the loam
and try again

February

the dead reeds are singing
snap a finger   they cannot feel it   what a perfect
shade of
off-white   this landscape so creamy

I want to trust them
to close my eyes and fall back and be caught in soft
embrace
the reeds are liars   they'll let me drop like
those ███ at school   the dead can't sing   but listen
          to the chaff
soothing twenty-year sorrow   quite literally saying
          hush
on repeat   take a handful clench   no pain
just a subdued arch   among lethean tides of noise
          pull and embers throb   at roots
her hair in a fist   her hair released into the wind
silent yet recall how it writhed with shame

          dancing dead

a pond in a school courtyard   filled with frogspawn and
reeds
          frogs fucking
with wild abandon   watched by hundreds of girls
screaming their prescribed disgust
          reeds hushing
calm down   said the swagger of the science block

looming over us   shoe of male genius bias
      pressing

I want to fall back and be caught

a courtyard in a hospital   filled with acheronian swill
      no pond
the doctors are kind but firm: the dead aren't rising
maddening whir of fans
stink of canteen grease   unspoken radius of space

weekly a girl would leap over the glassy void and fall
in
despite the hundreds that made it

     our cruel delight

half an orbit   stalking this river
drawn to brittle fingers
their persisting lament   clutching still to last
summer

observing perennial turn   wetlands swelling
     birds migrating

the quiet biology
of a crone lingering   flower   – lungwort –
between forefinger and thumb   rubbing

Cave

Your delicate tongue exposed, longing to quell
the thirst of millennia. Ensconced in ribcage cave,
my eyes lift another layer from your form.

You survived because you were lost to us.
Ochre submission no barricade to touch.

But the stag in striking obsidian is gentle, reverent.
Supplicates as though each member of the herd resides
within. You are life, blooded birth. Ochre resplendence.

Guilt: the realisation that the vulnerability
of our babes' also shrouds their young. A mother
skittering after us, searching for her child.

Atrocities of civilisation – expected trajectory
for an animal who has slain with connection laid bare.
Feasting on those we worship fucks you up

down the generational line. Minds capable of such duality,
surging through mutations that dislodge us from the web.

Red chalk of time, rhythm of breath, stuttering heartbeat.
In this swaddling of stone, dust bath of ablution, we may revert.

Something primal remains.

Acknowledgments:

I would like to thank Joel Evenden for his eternal support,
Nanci Lynch for always believing in me,
and Elizabeth Chadwick-Pywell for her keen eye and feedback.

Toil was originally published in *The Babel Tower Notice Board*,
Unearthed in *Jaden Magazine*, and *Barren* in *Porridge*.

Lightning Source UK Ltd.
Milton Keynes UK
UKHW011826191122
412485UK00005B/41